KOREN

In the Wild

Books by Edward Koren

Very Hairy Harry (2003)
Quality Time: Parenting, Progeny and Pets (1997)
What About Me? Cartoons from the New Yorker (1989)
Caution: Small Ensembles (1983)
The Penguin Edward Koren (1982)
Well, There's Your Problem (1980)
Are You Happy? And Other Questions Lovers Ask (1978)
Do You Want to Talk About It? (1976)
Behind the Wheel (1972)
Don't Talk to Strange Bears (1969)

Books Illustrated by Edward Koren

Cooking for Crowds by Merry White (2014)
Poems I Wrote When No One Was Looking by Alan Katz (2011)
How to Clean Your Room by Jennifer LaRue Huget (2010)
Oops! Poems by Alan Katz (2008)
Thelonius Monster's Sky-High Fly Pie by Judy Sierra (2006)
New Legal Seafoods Cookbook by Roger Berkowitz and Jane Doerfer (2003)
Pet Peeves or Whatever Happened to Doctor Rawf? by George Plimpton (2000)
All Together Now: a Y2K Program for Personal and Neighborhood Self-Reliance (1999)
The Hard Work of Simple Living: A Somewhat Blank Book for the Sustainable Hedonist (1998)
Dear Bruno by Alice Trillin (1996)
A Dog's Life by Peter Mayle (1996)
Do I Have to Say Hello? With Delia Ephron (1989)
Teenage Romance, or How to Die of Embarrassment with Delia Ephron (1982)
How to Eat Like a Child with Delia Ephron (1978)
Dragons Hate to Be Discreet by Winifred Rose (1978)
Noodles Galore by Merry White (1976)

In the Wild

Preface by Howard Norman
Appreciation by Ben Cohen, co-founder of Ben & Jerry's

BUTTON STREET PRESS NEWFANE, VERMONT

Button Street Press
Newfane, Vermont
www.buttonstreetpress.com

Drawings © 2018 Ed Koren
Preface © Howard Norman
Appreciation © Ben Cohen
Author photograph © Jon Gilbert Fox

All drawings in this collection originally appeared in *The New Yorker* and were published in the years 1966 through 2017 inclusive by
The New Yorker Magazine, Inc.

Design by Margot Mayor and Kitty Werner

Trade paper ISBN 978-1-939767-18-9
Hardcover ISBN 978-1-939767-19-6

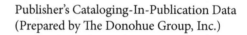

Publisher's Cataloging-In-Publication Data
(Prepared by The Donohue Group, Inc.)

Names: Koren, Edward, author. | Norman, Howard A., writer of supplementary textual content. | Cohen, Ben (Ben R.), writer of supplementary textual content.
Title: Koren : in the wild / [Edward Koren] ; preface by Howard Norman ; appreciation by Ben Cohen, co-founder of Ben & Jerry's.
Other Titles: In the wild | New Yorker (New York, N.Y. : 1925)
Description: Newfane, Vermont : Button Street Press, [2018] | "All drawings in this collection originally appeared in The New Yorker and were published in the years 1966 through 2014 inclusive by The New Yorker Magazine, Inc."
Identifiers: ISBN 9781939767189 (trade paperback) | ISBN 9781939767196 (hardcover)
Subjects: LCSH: Koren, Edward. | Country life--Caricatures and cartoons. | Caricatures and cartoons--United States.
Classification: LCC NC1429.K62 A4 2018 | DDC 741.5/973--dc23

TO MY BELOVED MATE CURTIS
TO MY DEAR KIDS AND THEIR MATES—
NAT/DEBORAH, SASHA/JESSAMIN,
BEN/ISABEL
TO MY GRAND DELIGHTS—ROSALIE AND ANNALISA
AND TO THE MEMORY OF MY FURRY MUSE,
CATMANDU
ALL MY DEVOTION—OF HEART AND MIND AND
DRAWING HAND

Ben Cohen and Ed Koren

An Appreciation from Ben Cohen

I've known Ed Koren for some 37 wonderful years, and we've bonded with our families and friends as we've carried out our lives in Vermont. Like Ed, I'm a Jewish guy from the suburbs of New York City, and, also like Ed, I've found my perfect place in Vermont, a place just about the opposite of New York City. I think both of us have done some of our best work inspired by our adopted state, appreciating its beauty and challenges and lovely quirks. It is a pleasure for me to call Ed a fellow Vermonter.

I came to Vermont because I got my first real job nearby, teaching crafts to emotionally disturbed teenagers at a school in the Adirondacks. On my days off, I'd go with other staff members to Burlington, the city closest to us.

I taught crafts for three years, and then tried to transition to being a full-time potter. But nobody bought my pots, so I joined the ranks of unsuccessful potters. Meanwhile, Jerry, who I grew up with in Merrick, Long Island, wanted to go to medical school, but he didn't get in.

We weren't really going anywhere, so we decided to start a business together, in Saratoga Springs, New York, where I had done a stint at Skidmore College — and where I met Curtis Ingham (Ed's future wife) who was in my film and jewelry classes. We used to hang out over frozen fondue dinners we heated up late at night over the Bunsen burners in the jewelry lab.

Jerry and I decided to make ice cream, but no one in Saratoga was much interested. So we moved to Burlington because we liked the city, and the scale of the place.

Ben & Jerry's would never have happened if we hadn't been in Vermont. We decided to use the tagline Vermont's Finest All Natural Ice Cream, an easy claim to make since there wasn't any other all-natural ice cream in Vermont. We couldn't have made the same claim in New York. In Vermont, we could be a big fish in a little pond. And we could become friends with the likes of Ed Koren, the second Cartoonist Laureate in Vermont — the only state that is forward-thinking enough to *have* a cartoonist laureate.

I met Ed, Curtis's paramour, in 1982, when I was just getting started in

Vermont in the ice cream business, and Ed and Curtis saw my picture on a pint of Ben & Jerry's. They got in touch to invite me to their wedding in Brookfield, and we've been friends ever since. Of course I had known Ed's work in *The New Yorker* magazine — back then, the cartoons were my main reason for reading *The New Yorker*.

For years, I had loved Ed's fuzzy and creative humanoid characters, his sense of humor and his subject matter. We have similar backgrounds, and I bonded with his sensibility.

Ed and Curtis's wedding featured a bunch of kids walking in before the bride and groom, carrying wooden posts holding three-foot-high colored drawings of flowers and fuzzy animals Ed had made — a sort of cheerleader's squad to herald the arrival of the bride and groom-to-be. One kid carried a huge ice cream cone with humanoid eyes and a goofy smile. I was moved by that, and Ed gave it to me. It's been framed and on my wall at home ever since.

We've stayed in touch, Ed and Curtis and I, hanging out in their backyard, or over dinners in their farmhouse kitchen, and celebrating this or that milestone in each other's lives. I try never to miss one of Curtis and Ed's celebrations or dinners or parties because they are always populated with so many amazing and fascinating and creative people, and also feature really good food.

After Jerry and I set up our business in Vermont, I never had any desire to be anywhere else. I felt — and feel — entirely at home here; I love the informal, down-home way of life, the working farms of all sorts all over the state, and the way Vermont maintains a farm ethic of thrift and common-sense and make-do. It's a place that encourages creativity.

I think a big part of the devotion to Vermont and the ethos that has developed in and about the State has to do with the fact that so much of the place is related to nature — the mountains, forests, rolling hills, farmland, rivers, the Lake — whereas in cities the revered places are man-made. Human beings are the major power in the city, while nature rules in the country.

I know Ed is devoted to Vermont, and it suits him. Ed is the only volunteer fireman I know personally, and I admire that. Being in Vermont also seems to suit his work schedule. When I call and get Ed on the phone, I can tell that he's at his drawing board, doing his many pen strokes. I can't hear his scribbles exactly, but I know he's sketching, sketching until he passes me off to Curtis, the Appointments Secretary, so we can plan our gatherings of all sorts.

One of the most amazing things about Vermont is its small scale, which I know appeals to Ed, too. It makes people and places accessible. Anyone can meet up with their local representatives in the VT legislature, or your Senator or Congressperson or Governor if you want to. The scale also makes it possible to bring innovative ideas to life.

Back when we decided to raise money at Ben & Jerry's with a new form of public stock offering, I just drove to Montpelier and easily met with the Commissioner of Banking and Insurance, who was mostly an amateur actor on the side. What we were proposing had never been done before — a public stock offering open only to Vermonters. He said, hey, good idea, and spent time showing me how to do a self-underwritten stock offering. That was an entirely new way of doing business, and Vermont's small scale made it work.

It has also given Ed brilliant access to the people and places that appear in so much of his work, as have his daily rural pleasures like outdoor chores and bike riding and cross-country skiing.

Ed, originally a city guy, now lives in a very rural village in Vermont. His cartoons beautifully capture the duality of rural and urban life. He's got Vermonters looking at city folk, and city folk looking at Vermonters.

For a guy like me, also between Vermont and New York, I love and can relate to Ed's humor, and to his humanoid and warm and fuzzy and puzzled and brave creatures. I consider it to be serendipitous, and my very good fortune, that we both ended up friends, which can easily happen in Vermont.

Ben Cohen
July 2018

"Do you ever miss New York?"

Preface by Howard Norman

"I can't quite get the frown right."

At one of our frequent dinners together, I mentioned to Ed Koren that I
think of him as a contrapuntalist. Because for six or so decades Koren, in
his inimitable cartoons, has so frequently penned a duet between disparate
philosophies of life: rural and urban.

More specifically, he puts on high exhibit the comportment of the denizens
of Vermont and New York, the two places that comprise Koren's most intimate
demographic (though I must add Paris, which provides Koren a kind of cultural
adrenalin). One might say that Koren is quintessentially local — and yet in
equal measure cosmopolitan. At age 83, he continues to apprentice himself to
his home-grown eccentric turns of mind.

I often get the sense that for days on end, Ed's humans and creatures are his preferred social life. I find this enviable, perhaps even part of an ancient hermetic tradition. Anyway, Koren has not only traveled widely in Brookfield village, but is so worldly, he can — while serving on the volunteer fire crew, or while on marathon bicycle treks, or just trying to figure out how to work a new-fangled espresso machine in his and Curtis's light-filled kitchen — mutter *sotto voce* in fluent French!

On occasion in a Koren cartoon, when one person offers a snippet of dubious wisdom, a capricious witticism, or a comment replete with curmudgeonly certitude, another person smiles (perhaps with hapless optimism) and yet another frowns (perhaps with abject glumness).

Contrapuntal responses!

"Cliches or ritual acts that annoy or amuse me or intrigue me are points of entry that allow me to construct small dramas," Koren wrote, "frozen in time and space, that people will laugh at (because they might have recognized themselves), and that I do laugh at (because I have recognized myself")."

What a splendid, autobiographical description of a cartoon.

This is not the place for a discussion of Edward Koren's career. We already know he is a cosmic observer and eavesdropper. We already know he is a sagacious chronicler of our hubris, our fraught complacency, and the luxurious problem of our existential angst.

We already comprehend that he is the great visual dramaturge of the human condition. To paraphrase Virginia Woolf, the trouble with life, is that our dreams are interrupted by our waking in the *media res* of a new day. True enough, but in *media res* is precisely where we encounter Koren's menagerie — open *The New Yorker* to a Koren cartoon, and you immediately partake of an incident of eternal gossip, a highbrow or lowbrow confab, verbal slapstick, or even the comic gravitas of quotidian life.

And let's face it, Koren gives us the hard truth — people are quite capable of saying just about anything to each other.

In interviews and conversation, Koren readily speaks of how the art of his mentors, and his chosen aesthetic coterie, perpetually informs and inspires his own work. These include – to combine centuries here — Daumier, Thurber, Arno, Steinberg, and George Herriman. Yet Koren is that rarest of creatures,

a true ORIGINAL. (Regarding Ed's modesty, picture a Korenesque figure, dejectedly slumped in a chair in front of his work desk, saying to his wife standing in the doorway, "I've just realized that I'm not *sui generis*.")

As for posterity, the legions of us Korenophiles, along with future scholars of the Koren Era, will eventually be able to experience the whole prodigious shebang — drafts, emendations, sketchbooks, finished drawings, *New Yorker* cartoons and covers, and more — in the Billy Ireland Cartoon Library and Museum, at the Ohio State University, in Columbus, Ohio. It will prove a dignified testimony to a working life that so dignified art.

At the Kellogg Hubbard Library's celebration of Ed, I said that it was my firm belief that — in concert with his original authorship of hundreds of captions, and his finely-tuned ear for "linguistically encapsulated foibles," (how Edward Lear referred to the transmuting of overheard sentences into captions) — Ed Koren magically induces people within his proximity to utter outlandish things. He *causes* this to happen. Of course, this is a subjective theory and can't be proven; still, allow me some anecdotal evidence.

One winter afternoon, I met Ed in the cafeteria of the Metropolitan Museum of Art in New York. He had come in out of the cold, and the very moment he sat at our table (after sizing up the romantic couple at the next table), a young woman reached across to place her hand over the hand of a young man, and said,

"Thomas, tell me everything you know about food." Hearing this, Ed merely shrugged, took out his notebook, made a quick sketch and jotted down, "Tell me everything you know about food." (It is nice to witness the birth a caption.)

One evening, Ed and I were sitting at a table at the Three Penny Taproom in Montpelier. The waitress had just described "tonight's special." It was some sort of out sized Reuben-like sandwich, served with fries. Ed was intrigued and ordered it. Next to us sat a late middle age couple, who felt the need to inform us that they lived on the Upper West Side of New York. When the waitress set Ed's meal on the table, the man of the New York couple leaned close, and promoting the obvious as a revelation, exclaimed, "I see you ordered

the special." Out came the notebook. Ed's narrative imagination thus incited: on the notebook page appeared two shaggy Korenesque men sitting at dinner. Well over the confines of a plate, sprawled one of Koren's decidedly mesozoic creatures (with expressive hands) who, though clearly dead, still maintained a bemused expression. The aforementioned male New York interloper spoke the caption: "I see you've ordered the special." I rest my case.

The great maestro of Yiddish prose, Sholom Aleichem wrote, "My village is full of well-meaning, or not so well-meaning souls who can't help what rolls off their tongues. Why else, wherever I go day and night, would I carry my pen and my journal full of empty pages with their insatiable loneliness?"

My family's farmhouse was built circa 1850. The upstairs guest room is called The Koren Room. If five hundred years from now an archaeologist attempts to decipher how we lived, said archaeologist would find an archive of certain rites-of-passage of our tribe, framed celebrations on paper drawn by the 20th and 21st century iconic cartoonist Edward Koren.

Because in a very basic sense, Koren, for many of his friends, becomes a kind of family historian. The wedding announcement. The birth-of-a-daughter announcement. Numerous announcements denoting the Passage of Time, such as birthdays and anniversaries. In fact, I would actually prefer a Koren representation on my gravestone. I have said this to Ed. What might this look like, he asked. I thought: a Korenesque figure looking flummoxed and yet also resigned. After the parenthetical birth-death dates, the epigraph (caption) might read: "I Just Knew This Would Happen."

It is quite easy for me to get into a fugue state of exuberance about Edward Koren's drawings, cartoons, lithographs, everything everything everything.

What a full life. He speaks French so well, too! (When down in the dumps, I have, on occasion, requested that Ed do his uncanny, hyperbolic imitation of a Quebecois hockey announcer).

Above all, Koren works hard. We share a fondness for something the artist Chuck Close said, "Amateurs wait for inspiration, while the restof us just get up and go to work." Unless there is hard work at one's art, unless the artist experiences endless resistance to perfection, the mind has no base from which to rise, nor does the heart.

I remember this one time when I visited the organized chaos of Ed's studio, (the somnambulist's lair — Ed is something of a nocturnal creature) and looked at an in-progress full-sized cartoon promised to *The New Yorker*. The setting was the interior of an airplane filled with passengers. Some arresting announcement or other had just been delivered by intercom — or was it from a flight attendant? To my untrained eye the drawing was perfection. But Ed pointed to a figure in the second row, and said, "I've been working on this for days and I can't quite get the frown right."

That spoke so classically, of course, about the life of the serious artist— to not ever take one's relationship with one's muse for granted, passion, obsessiveness and craft, and finally, the holding of a frown at the highest level of regard, as you don't want to allow something unfinished into the world.

Life is hard. Oh beloved contrapuntalist, Edward Koren, thank you for such blessed reprieves from sadness, from the ghastly incursion of mortality. For hay wagons full of laughter.

These are wonderful cartoons.

Howard Norman

"Do you know how much I love you?"

"I know it's hard to believe, but this is a great Beaujolais town."

"You hate to shop—I hate to hunt."

"Do you have lunch plans?"

"I don't feel like going out. Why don't just the two of us stay in and open a can of worms?"

"Love you!"

"If you can stand the cuteness, take a look at my cat."

"We're only here summers, but Roger likes to be taken for a local."

"All right, food people—are you ready?"

"I need everybody to come down to the garden to cheer on the tomatoes."

"We live a few miles from here in an architecturally significant former gas station."

"Here's some baby spinach—from my soil to your plate."

"Hey, Johnny—am I nuts, or does this have a hint of oak?"

"No, you're not too late. Cathy's just beginning
to put calcium into perspective."

"And where did you put the rest of the moose?"

"I'd like my daughter to know something about engines."

"Daniel has become indifferent to weather conditions."

*"I'm never bored! I've got my pottery, my plants,
my weaving, and my man."*

"When the children have all grown up, we hope to move back to the city."

"That's my mom and dad. They've just returned to traditional family values."

"These are some of my new friends from the birthing class."

"Zero population growth!"

"This is a great place to bring up children."

"Your father and I want to explain why we've decided to live apart."

"I know I haven't been much of a master to you, but then again
you haven't been much of a pet to me."

"I hear you enjoy tinkering."

"Hugh understands wood."

"Hey—this is the quiet trail!"

"Great fall, Josh!"

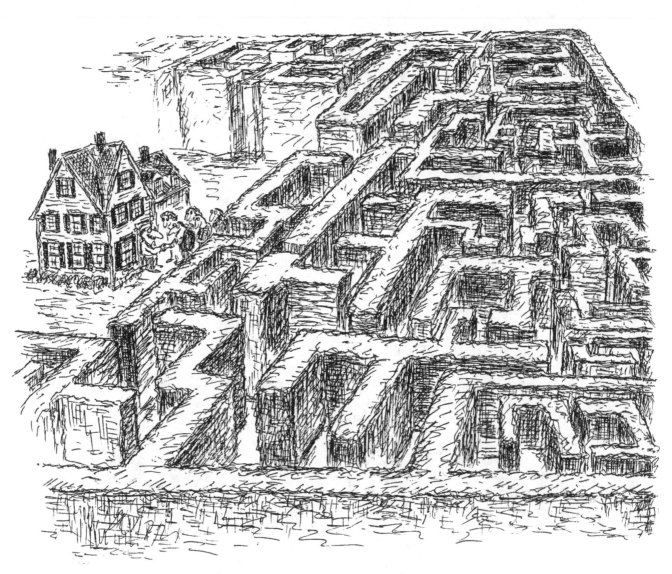

"Your instructions were perfect."

"Carol, our guests are here, along with the entire L.L. Bean catalogue!"

"Look what I found yesterday when we were cleaning out the attic."

"And this? Trash or treasure?"

*"I spent most of my time this summer gardening and cooking,
and Charles answered his mail."*

"Well, for _your_ information, I happen to _love_ nature."

"Come, join me for a few moments of mindful indolence!

"Will you share my dream with me, Alexandra? A few acres somewhere,
a couple of sheep, a couple of pigs, some chickens ..."

ANOTHER
BEAUTIFUL
HISTORIC HOUSE
WAITING
TO BE
RESTORED
Providence Preservation Society

"There are some words I will not tolerate in this house—and 'awesome' is one of them."

"For the last time—Daddy doesn't do sports."

"Happy?"

"I've been a great admirer of your work for years. It's a real pleasure to meet you."

"I'm happy to meet _you_. I'm your biggest fan."

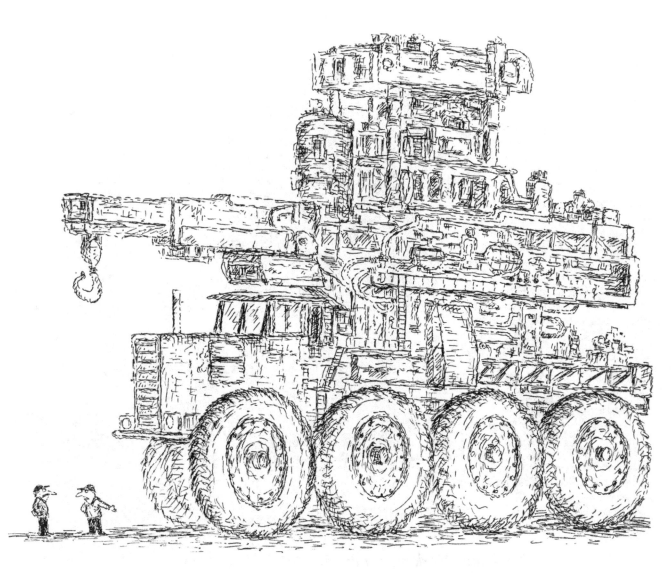

"She's on the blink."

"You know, Mark, your tabouli salad makes us look bad."

"Kate, this is the wonderful man I told you about who has such a strong hand with garlic and fresh thyme."

"Give me a whiskey with a shot of wheatgrass,
ginger, beet, and local honey."

"We think it's terribly important that you meet the people responsible for the food you're eating tonight."

"I don't own a wood stove. I burn oil!"

"And on my right is Joe Nast, representing an opposing viewpoint."

"May I join your rumination group?"

"I'm indoorsy and Paul is outdoorsy."

"Can I call you back? Jim and I are struggling with our roles."

"What, may I ask, does landscape have to do with gender?"

"Any Impressionists in this crowd?"

"So <u>this</u> is the famous Sarah of the mustard-mayonnaise clam dip!"

"Since the food you serve is not organically grown, is it safe to assume that the meat is laced with antibiotics and the salad is chockful of pesticides?"

"I love this planet!"

"Off to meditation?"

"Really, Susan! I never thought of you as the hysterical type."

90

"What's scrumptious?"

"And now for the taste test."

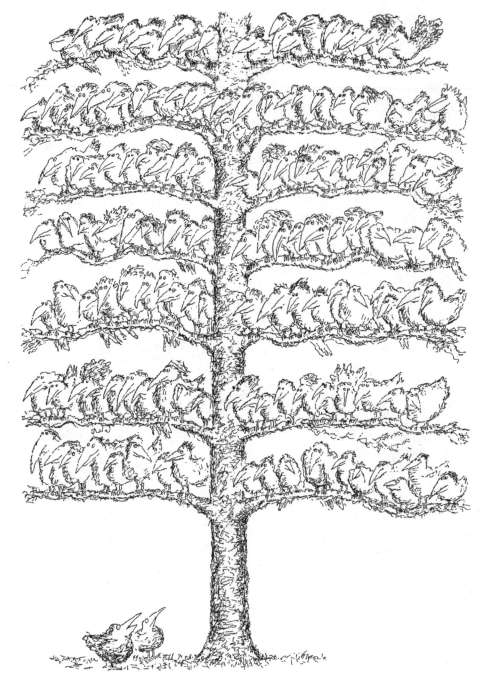

"See anyone you know?"

"She's family."

"Our philosophy here at Dandelion Motors is to treat the total car."

"I've <u>done</u> my tour of duty on Wall Street."

"Honey, are you thinking about the office?"

"I'm a fresh-vegetable fan."

"Are you a hunter or a food gatherer?"

"Well, <u>there's</u> your problem."

"Why not take her out for a spin? It'll blow your socks off."

"My friend, you are weighty in form but light in content."

"You grab the food—I'll grab the wine."

"I keep thinking about last night's salmon en croûte."

"Who can we call?"

"We're really bonding now, aren't we, Dad?"

"There's my very first school—where I learned how to hug."

"Hey—we just catch and release."

"Tell them how hard we've worked to protect their habitat."

"Oh, boy, hard-core sugar!"

"No more carbohydrates until you finish your protein."

"I work four hours in the morning. Then meditation and errands."

"I love this place—its food, its ambiance and its political goals."

"I'd like to tell you about our specials this evening."

"Why can't you be more supportive?"

"Carol—you're muttering about NPR again."

*"Often, it's sullen and withdrawn, and then, suddenly,
it becomes hostile and vengeful."*

"I want you to know I'm angry and hurt."

"Are you just pissing and moaning, or can you verify what you're saying with data?"

"I'm just getting around to sowing my wild oats."

"Could you fellas tell me if there's any place around
here where I could find a fax machine?"

"Well, it <u>has</u> been a great summer for chanterelles."

"How's my sweet little bugaboo?"

"Clark and Denise are our closest neighbors."

"We motored over to say hi!"

"Great for worship then! Great for retail now!"

"I think you'll find this home has real storybook charm."

"I thought I'd give Western medicine one more chance."

"Martin and I just bought sixty-five acres in Vermont, and as soon as we get around to building a house you must come up and visit."

"*It's a perfect day to reorganize those closets.*"

"Yes, I'm still getting up early, but these days it's good to check on the spot markets for oil and natural gas."

"I'm only a few miles from home. Could I borrow a socket?"

"It's a narrative I didn't intend."

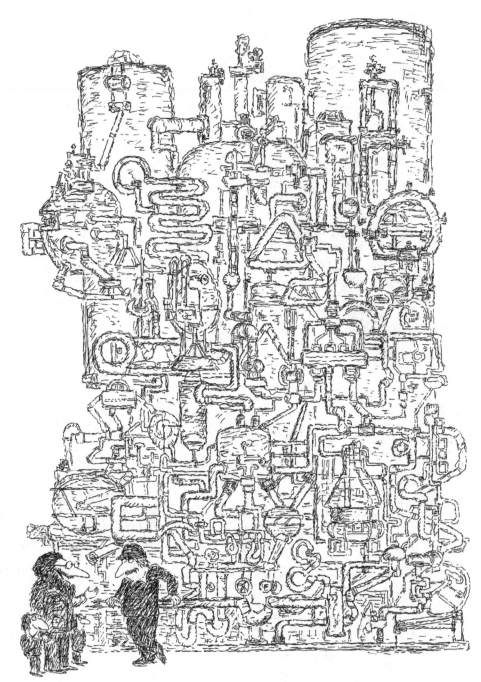

"Where's the business end of this thing?"

"We can't tell yet if it's a malfunction or a dysfunction."

"We want organic, we want local, and we want cruelty-free."

"I'm in the mood for meat."

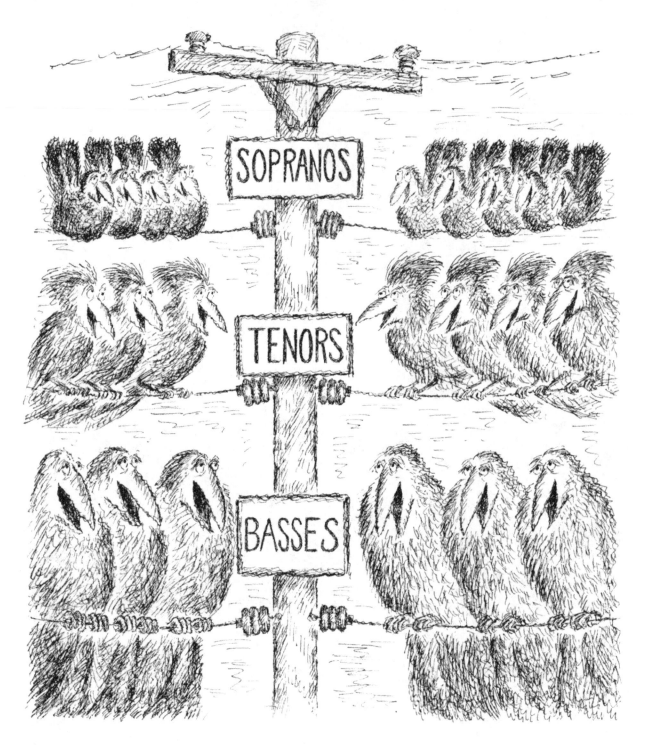

148

"Oh, excuse me! I thought you were somebody I know."

"I think Jules is reminding Nat that each and every one of us produces
four pounds of garbage each day, every day."

"We sing her to sleep with songs about recycling."

"I __never__ think about cholesterol when I'm on vacation."

"How far is two pounds from here?"

"You're terrific, Katia. You think like 'The New York Review of Books' and look like 'Vogue.'"

"My darling, I want to share my money worries, my tensions, and my unhappiness with you for the rest of my life."

"Philip has said everything there is to say."

"Don is an intellectual _and_ a regular guy."

"Rufus, come on! We're doing this as a family!"

"Please—stand by me forever!"

"The word you're searching for is 'wife.'"

"I want to cry, because I'm so happy."

"Isn't this <u>fun</u>?"

"You're a hard act to follow."

"Would you like to scratch my back?"

"*He loves to be petted.*"

"He's a very fussy eater."

"Now, this is a very new variety, which some people are having trouble relating to."

"How old is your cabbage?"

"<u>Now</u> what?"

"Your bell sounds lovely this evening."

"Great set of pipes!"

"From a man's point of view do you think it's beautiful?"

"At great personal risk, I'd like to compliment you on your perfume."

"Great news! 'Tarzan' is out in paperback!"

"Everything's just fine. The garden is coming in beautifully,
and Jeremy is in his usual rage."

"Oh, there's Freddie. He knows the best places to suffer."

"Jonathan is associate professor of soups and salads at our local culinary institute."

"The service is polite and well meaning, if a little slow."

"Jerry, I'm beginning to think it's wrong that all our fun
is based on the combustion of hydrocarbons."

"We found the most marvelous little place where they sell gasoline."

"Ah, Hopkins! <u>Finalmente!</u>"

"I'm having my annual reunion with Polartec, Thinsulate, fleece, and my oldest friend, wool."

"This is my wife, Katerina, formerly of Bloomingdales's."

"The weather looks a little iffy."

SCENIC
AREA

189

"Isn't it astonishing that no two of us are exactly alike?"

"Quick! Get your gun, Pa! Here come the suburbs."

About the Author

Edward Koren has long been associated with the *The New Yorker* magazine, where he has published over 1100 cartoons, as well as numerous covers and illustrations. He has also contributed to many other publications, written and illustrated several books for children, and illustrated many more in various genres.

Born in New York City, Koren attended the Horace Mann School and Columbia University. He did graduate work in etching and engraving with S.W. Hayter at Atelier 17 in Paris, and received an M.F.A. degree from Pratt Institute. He was on the faculty of Brown University for many years.

Koren's cartoons, drawing and prints have been widely exhibited in shows across the United States as well as in France, England and Czechoslovakia. A major retrospective of his work was shown at Columbia University's Wallach Gallery in 2010, and at the University of Vermont's Fleming Museum in the summer of 2011.

Koren has deep roots in both New York City and Vermont, where he lives with his family and has been a member of the Brookfield VT Volunteer Fire Dept for 30 years. In 2007 he received The Vermont Governor's Award for Excellence in the Arts, and served a three-year term as Vermont's second Cartoonist Laureate (Vermont is the only state in the nation with a Cartoonist Laureate.)

New York and Vermont intertwine in Ed's life and work, where he gleefully practices his exquisite talent for noticing. As he writes in his Artist Notes about his exhibition at Columbia University: "What captures my attention is all the human theater around me. I can never quite believe my luck in stumbling upon riveting mini-dramas taking place within earshot (and eyeshot), a comedy of manners that seems inexhaustible. And to be always undercover makes my practice of deep noticing even more delicious. I can take in all the details as long as I appear inattentive — false mustache and dark glasses I place. All kinds of wonderful moments of comedy happen right under my nose. My low expectations are never disappointed, or, as Lily Tomlin has observed, "No matter how cynical I get, I can never keep up."

CPSIA information can be obtained
at www.ICGtesting.com
Printed in the USA
BVHW011431210519
548840BV00003B/5/P